Too Cute!
Baby Seals

by Elizabeth Neuenfeldt

BELLWETHER MEDIA
MINNEAPOLIS, MN

Blastoff! Beginners are developed by literacy experts and educators to meet the needs of early readers. These engaging informational texts support young children as they begin reading about their world. Through simple language and high frequency words paired with crisp, colorful photos, Blastoff! Beginners launch young readers into the universe of independent reading.

Sight Words in This Book

a	is	this
at	it	time
eat	look	to
get	more	up
have	the	will
in	they	with

This edition first published in 2024 by Bellwether Media, Inc.

No part of this publication may be reproduced in whole or in part without written permission of the publisher. For information regarding permission, write to Bellwether Media, Inc., Attention: Permissions Department, 6012 Blue Circle Drive, Minnetonka, MN 55343.

Library of Congress Cataloging-in-Publication Data

Names: Neuenfeldt, Elizabeth, author.
Title: Baby seals / Elizabeth Neuenfeldt.
Description: Minneapolis, MN : Bellwether Media, 2024. | Series: Blastoff! Beginners: Too Cute! | Includes bibliographical references and index. | Audience: Ages 4-7 | Audience: Grades K-1
Identifiers: LCCN 2023039881 (print) | LCCN 2023039882 (ebook) | ISBN 9798886877731 (library binding) | ISBN 9798886878677 (ebook)
Subjects: LCSH: Seals (Animals)--Infancy--Juvenile literature.
Classification: LCC QL737.P64 N48 2024 (print) | LCC QL737.P64 (ebook) | DDC 599.79/139--dc23 eng/20230825
LC record available at https://lccn.loc.gov/2023039881
LC ebook record available at https://lccn.loc.gov/2023039882

Text copyright © 2024 by Bellwether Media, Inc. BLASTOFF! BEGINNERS and associated logos are trademarks and/or registered trademarks of Bellwether Media, Inc.

Editor: Betsy Rathburn   Designer: Jeffrey Kollock

Printed in the United States of America, North Mankato, MN.

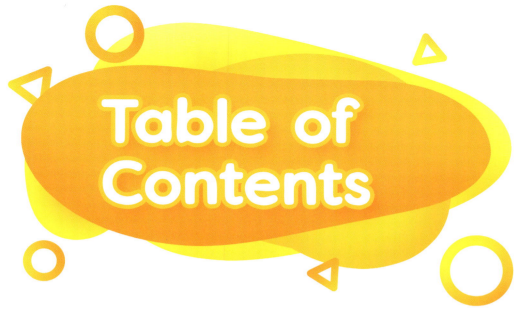

Table of Contents

A Baby Seal!	4
Close to Mom	6
All Grown Up!	16
Baby Seal Facts	22
Glossary	23
To Learn More	24
Index	24

A Baby Seal!

Look at the baby seal. Hello, pup!

Close to Mom

Newborn pups have fur.
It is very soft!

fur

Pups live in **colonies**.

colony

They stay close to mom. They drink mom's milk.

mom

Pups sleep a lot.
They cuddle mom.

They swim with mom.
They dive deep!

All Grown Up!

Pups get bigger. They spend more time alone.

They learn
to hunt.
They eat fish.

Pups grow up fast.
This pup will
get even bigger!

Baby Seal Facts

Seal Life Stages

newborn　　　pup　　　adult

A Day in the Life

drink mom's milk　　　swim　　　hunt

Glossary

colonies

large groups of seals

newborn

just born

To Learn More

ON THE WEB

FACTSURFER

Factsurfer.com gives you a safe, fun way to find more information.

1. Go to www.factsurfer.com.

2. Enter "baby seals" into the search box and click 🔍.

3. Select your book cover to see a list of related content.

Index

alone, 16
colonies, 8, 9
cuddle, 12
dive, 14
drink, 10
eat, 18
fish, 18
fur, 6
grow, 20

hunt, 18
milk, 10
mom, 10, 11, 12, 14
newborn, 6, 7
seal, 4
sleep, 12
swim, 14

The images in this book are reproduced through the courtesy of: COULANGES, front cover, p. 1; Nicram Sabod, pp. 3, 6; Malyshev1974, p. 4; Robert Haasmann, p. 5; Nature Picture Library/ Alamy, pp. 7, 15; Erwin Niemand, p. 9; Paul Thompson Live News/ Alamy, p. 11; Erin Donalson, p. 13; kubais, p. 14; blickwinkel/ Alamy, pp. 17, 21; Arterra Picture Library/ Alamy, p. 19; Darnell, Sarah/ SuperStock, p. 22 (newborn); Vladimir Melnik, p. 22 (pup); slowmotiongli, p. 22 (adult); Mark Williams/ Alamy, p. 22 (drink milk); Anneka, p. 22 (swim); Agencja Fotograficzna Caro/ Alamy, p. 22 (hunt); marcobrivio.photography, p. 23 (colonies); Dave Hunt/ Alamy, p. 23 (newborn).